Gettin' Poetic Down Under

by Heather Jane Hill

Gettin' Poetic Down Under
© 2025 Heather Jane Hill
Published in Australia by Heather Jane Hill 2025
This collection of words belongs to the author.
Please share with heart, not with copy-paste.
Contact: Heather Jane Hill, c/- Moonta Post Office, S.A. 5558.
Facebook: https://www.facebook.com/profile.php?id=61581776847480
All rights reserved.
No part of this publication may be reproduced, distributed, or
transmitted in any form or by any means, including photocopying,
recording, or other electronic or mechanical methods, without the prior
written permission of the author, except in the case of brief quotations
embodied in critical reviews and certain other noncommercial uses
permitted by copyright law.
Disclaimer: The Dunlop Volley Odes is an independent work of poetry and
literary expression. Beyond our contact in the 1990s during the writing of these
poems, this book is not sponsored by, or reflective of, Brand Collective or the
Dunlop Volley brand today.

For John and Thelma

Dad, you gave me tenacity and a sense of humour.
Mum, you gave me creativity and smarts.
Thanks for ski lessons, finance, reading to me, and chocolate cake!
I love you both so very much.

Contents   Page Number

Aging	1
All That Truly Matters	3
Australia is a Dangerous Place	5
Copper and Blood	9
Jack and Jill—*North Queensland Style*	11
Jack and Jill—*South Australian Style*	15
Parenthood	19
Red Lid	20
The Legend of the Windbreaker Three	24
The Lump	28
The Power of Wind	33
Things Life Gave You	35
Unmoored	37
Winter at the Station	39
The Dunlop Volley Odes	41
Ode to a Dunlop Volley	44
Ode to a Missing Volley	47
Ode to a Volley's Twilight Hour	49
Ode to the Resurrection of the Gripping Volley	51
Ode to Roofers Too Sexy for their Volleys	53

Let words communicate and empower,
    as words should—
        be they written,
            spoken,
                or gestured.

Contents   Page Number

Aging	1
All That Truly Matters	3
Australia is a Dangerous Place	5
Copper and Blood	9
Jack and Jill—*North Queensland Style*	11
Jack and Jill—*South Australian Style*	15
Parenthood	19
Red Lid	20
The Legend of the Windbreaker Three	24
The Lump	28
The Power of Wind	33
Things Life Gave You	35
Unmoored	37
Winter at the Station	39
The Dunlop Volley Odes	41
Ode to a Dunlop Volley	44
Ode to a Missing Volley	47
Ode to a Volley's Twilight Hour	49
Ode to the Resurrection of the Gripping Volley	51
Ode to Roofers Too Sexy for their Volleys	53

Let words communicate and empower,
as words should—
be they written,
spoken,
or gestured.

Aging

Children pass me daily
they make their way to school
throwing rocks
laughing
why must they be so cruel?
I lean like a drunkard
I squeak and I moan
but this old rustic cottage
was once a family home.

When flora and fauna fall,
>   the earth reclaims them.
When we fall,
>   the earth rejects our waste.

All That Truly Matters

Sunset cloaks the forest range
a silhouette in song.
Birds cry out a lullaby
sharp echoes loud and long.

Among the rocks the hunters wake
night's veil conceals their eyes.
They prowl for food—for sustenance
beneath the darkened skies.

Survival is the only goal
to live another day,
not vanish in the forest deep
as silent, helpless prey.

As humans, we're no different
we battle through each day—
for place, for bread, for treasure,
the richest hold the sway.

But creatures of the forest
take only what they need,
while humankind, insatiable
is driven forth by greed.

Will we ever find satisfaction
or learn a wiser wealth,
when all that truly matters here
is life, and love, and health?

FUN FACT: There are many dangers in Australia—some we might not even think of. As a rural-remote nurse, I've seen and treated many things firsthand:

Snake, lizard, tick and spider bites. Jellyfish and bullrout stings (freshwater stonefish). Crocodile attack injuries—freshwater ones, that is. One generally doesn't walk away from a saltwater crocodile attack! Freshies not only bite, but they also scratch.

And then there are stinging tree stings, mango tree sap reactions, hairy caterpillar rashes, and bee-sting allergies and anaphylaxis. Rafting injuries—heads don't fare well when slammed against rocks. Feral pig gores, slips on dangerous yet unassuming mossy rocks, and a whole lot more.

Grey nomads are a surprise. They slip off caravan steps regularly. The old steps were square, with unforgiving, sharp corners. The new ones are rounded and far less problematic.

The injury that surprised me most belonged to the tough, rugged, and usually aged farmer. The old farm utes, which have served them well for decades, rust in the tropical rain. Eventually, the day comes when the rust that holds the tailgate on can take no more—*voilà!*—shin flesh removed.

Knives were also a common cause of injury across all ages. Knives don't discriminate. Whether it's in the kitchen, on the boat, at work, or in the shed, those dangerous little suckers will slice a digit right off.

Australia is a Dangerous Place

"Australia is a dangerous place—everybody dies!"
An American tourist told me with sheer terror in her eyes.

"Crocodiles eat you—and sharks will do the same.
Jellyfish paralyse with excruciating pain!

"Ticks will suck your blood, leaving toxins as they go.
The giant, feathered cassowary disembowels with just one blow!

"Yes, snakes are slithering all around, most with fatal bites.
Your Amethystine Python crushes with its might!

"Spiders grow as big as hands—six inches long in length.
And rivers sweep you right away, with awesome flooding strength.

"Eating forest fruit can be a deadly thing to do.
If you don't stay familiar with what's good and bad for you.

"Roos bound through bush by night, and even some by day,
I see they try and box with you—a marsupial affray!

"Your bungy rope could snap on you. Your rafting boats collide.
If day-trip vessels hit the reef, they'd drown tourists inside.

"A skydiver's parachute could fail. Your hot air balloons go bang.
Get gored by a feral pig. Get hit by a boomerang.

Continues...

"A falling coconut can kill. You could slip down a waterfall.
Mosquitoes spread viruses. Giant lizards scratch and crawl!

"What about the stonefish? Sea snakes on the Reef?
Left behind on tour? Stung by a stinging leaf?

"Why would you want to live in such a God-forsaken place?
It's not fit for habitation by the human race."

I said, "I love it—cyclones, droughts—the fear and the excitement.
I've travelled and I wouldn't live on any other continent."

"But it's safer in the States," she said. I debated, "Bears and moose?
Overcrowded subways? Gunmen on the loose?

"Big cats, cobras, twisters, hurricanes, earthquakes in LA?
My heart beats green and gold," I said. "Australia's where I'll stay."

Kangaroos can't hop backwards.

How would they manage a Lawyer Vine entanglement?

As a practice nurse, I vaccinated children.
    Mothers sought my opinion.
        Often, it was to argue for or against.
But it wasn't my opinion that mattered.
    Better, the opinion of their forefathers—
        those who buried children, from disease.

The following poem is about my hometown, Moonta, South Australia, where copper was discovered in 1861 and mining followed. Moonta is located on traditional lands of the Nharangga people.

Copper and Blood

Simple folk—hope clutched in hands,
travelled for miles over heartless lands.
Through lifeless, salt-bush scattered plains,
Desert-cold nights, freezing-cold rains.

In heat that surpassed one hundred degrees,
no shade, no shelter, no water, no trees.
Lured by promise—unaware,
it would take more than toil and fervent prayer.

While men and boys worked the mines,
breathed the dust of broken fines.
In shanty homes, babes fell ill,
many passing—a bitter pill.

Graves unmarked for young and old,
blank pages in history—stories untold.
Their hardship, a sadness I can't comprehend,
an era long lived, now at its end.

As a nurse, I cared for an elderly man,
whose family, he said, mined this same land.
Brothers and sisters who he'd held dear,
had sadly been buried all in one year.

Tears welled in his eyes as I stood by his side,
the weight of the years, his loss and his pride.
I considered my past, born in good times,
I'd never know hardship, nor working in mines.

FUN FACT: The stinging tree leaf mentioned in the following poem comes from the Gympie-Gympie. The tree grows to around two metres tall and is found in the rainforests of eastern Australia. It has a heart-shaped leaf with a deceptively soft appearance.

During several decades working in tourism out of Cairns, I came across this painful beast regularly, both while leading guided walks and in emergencies.

Because it grows within easy reach and has broad, soft-looking leaves, it's often chosen for bush toilet paper. Tiny hairs on the leaf's surface lodge into the skin while wiping, and break off, releasing a potent neurotoxin. In some people, the sting can cause anaphylaxis.

The embedded hairs are removed by waxing the affected area. Treatment often requires a trip to the emergency department. As the hairs are microscopic, removal isn't always complete, and lingering pain can persist for days, weeks, and months. Bushwalkers are often stung on the limbs while brushing past, too.

Best you BYO toilet paper when it comes to going bush!

Jack and Jill—*North Queensland Style*

Jack and Jill went up the hill,
Mount Whitfield to be precise.
They got to the top and Jill spoke out,
"The view Jack, ain't it nice?"

But Jack stopped still and glared at Jill,
not noticing the view.
Instead, he clutched his stomach fast,
and said, "I need the loo!"

Jill glared back, mouth clenched tight,
hands folded a frustrated way.
"Why didn't you go when we left home?
You *always* spoil my day!"

Jill voiced, "There ain't a loo for miles,
that should be pretty clear."
But Jack just made a groaning sound,
fluffed, then shed a tear.

"I see ya desperate, brother Jack—
the only thing to do.
Is hurry behind them bushes, there,
for your face is turnin' blue!"

Jack ran into the thicket,
certain no one was in sight.
He dropped his dacks at breakneck pace,
then grinned in sheer delight.

Continues...

"Ah, that's better," sighed young Jack,
relieved to say the least.
"Good job I did it facin' west,
for the breeze is headed east!"

Jill stood downwind on the eastern side,
of where Jack chose to squat.
Her nose curled up accordingly,
"Boy d'ya stink, or what?

"I'm gettin' out'a here, dear Jack—
your gut is surely rotten?
I'm headin' down the hill right now,
I'll meet you at the bottom."

Jack didn't mind being left alone,
to finish what he'd started.
"I'll race you there, sister of mine!
I'll race you there," he chanted.

Then near to him, the bushes swayed,
a squatting Jack grew tense.
"Jill?" he growled, and eyed a leaf,
to wipe the evidence.

The leaf Jack eyed was heart in shape,
jagged-edged, broad, and pliable.
A clean bum it would guarantee,
its softness undeniable.

Jack reached out and picked that leaf,
but felt his heart rate rise.
A head came over his right shoulder,
to Jack's complete surprise!

Wattle red and neck of blue,
bony casque upon its head.
"A cassowary," trembled Jack,
remembering warnings read…

As slow as slow, Jack took that leaf,
wiped, then felt a twinge.
T'was from the ruthless stinging tree,
the leaf that made him cringe.

Jack jumped up, let out a squeal,
his dacks around his feet.
The cassowary—frightened now,
wasn't planning retreat.

Its head went down, its feathers fluffed,
its sharp toes kicked at Jack,
But Jack was running—pants still down,
he knew he was under attack.

Express route through ferns and trees,
no track did he require.
The stinging tree leaf had seen to that,
his rear almost on fire.

The cassowary lost poor Jack,
Jack was just too slick.
The boy arrived at the base of the hill,
with Jill approaching quick.

With poison in his butt crack,
a forced grin hid his pain.
He'd raced his sister down the hill,
and for that—he'd do it all again!

FUN FACT: Because I've spent my life between Tropical North Queensland and South Australia (my birthplace), I wrote two similar versions of *Jack and Jill* to be relevant to both northern and southern Australia.

Caltrop, which is mentioned in the following poem, is an introduced creeping weed from North Africa. It's toxic to livestock. Its burrs have four sharp spines—ouch!

Caltrops have been used as weapons throughout history, made from materials such as nails, steel and wrought iron. Three prongs offer support on the ground, while the fourth prong stands upright. That's the dangerous one!

Can you imagine fighting in an ancient or modern war and trying to cross terrain with these beauties strewn across it? They've even been made with barbs! Either way, they stop humans, horses and camels in their tracks.

Tubular steel caltrops are used today and made hollow to pierce and flatten tyres.

Just the name of the plant is enough to make you cringe!

The poems do start the same, but the ending differs.

Jack and Jill—*South Australian Style*

Jack and Jill went up the hill,
Mount Lofty to be precise.
They got to the top and Jill spoke out,
"The view Jack, ain't it nice?"

But Jack stopped still and glared at Jill,
not noticing the view.
Instead, he clutched his stomach fast,
and said, "I need the loo!"

Jill glared back, mouth clenched tight,
hands folded a frustrated way.
"Why didn't you go when we left home?
You *always* spoil my day!"

Jill voiced, "There ain't a loo for miles,
that should be pretty clear."
But Jack just made a groaning sound,
fluffed, then shed a tear.

"I see ya desperate, brother Jack—
the only thing to do.
Is hurry behind them bushes, there,
for your face is turnin' blue!"

Jack ran into the thicket,
certain no one was in sight.
He dropped his dacks at breakneck pace,
then grinned in sheer delight.

Continues...

"Ah, that's better," sighed young Jack,
relieved to say the least.
"Good job I did it facin' west,
for the breeze is headed east!"

Jill stood downwind on the eastern side,
of where Jack chose to squat.
Her nose curled up accordingly,
"Boy d'ya stink, or what?

"I'm gettin' out'a here, dear Jack—
your gut is surely rotten?
I'm headin' down the hill right now,
I'll meet you at the bottom."

Jack didn't mind being left alone,
to finish what he'd started.
"I'll race you there, sister of mine!
I'll race you there," he chanted.

Then near to him, the bushes swayed,
a squatting Jack grew tense.
"Jill?" he growled, and eyed a leaf,
to wipe the evidence.

The plant Jack eyed had grey-green leaves,
'twas fern-like across the ground.
He'd use the plant to wipe his bum,
and wouldn't make a sound.

Jack reached to grab a handful,
but felt his heart rate rise.
Two strong legs with talon feet—
an unexpected surprise.

Camouflaged by scrubland,
Jack hadn't seen the nest.
A clutch of blue-green emu eggs,
the father their defence.

Shaggy, grey-brown feathers shook,
sharp talons scraped the ground.
Jack's empty bowel yielded more,
and sprayed across the ground.

He swiped and wiped in one fell swoop,
escape was now a must.
He was running, pants now up,
the emu in his dust.

Through the trees and down the hill,
no track did he require.
Spiky Caltrop spines fixed that,
his rear almost on fire.

Old man emu quit the chase,
Jack was just too slick.
The boy arrived at the base of the hill,
with Jill approaching quick.

Despite spines in his butt crack,
a forced smile hid his pain.
He'd raced his sister down the hill,
and for that—he'd do it all again!

In Australia:
>> We are required to register our pets.
>> We are required to register our children.

Sometimes:
>> Pets are abused and mistreated.
>> Children are abused and mistreated.

To breed pets:
>> There are state and local government requirements.
>> To have children—no requirements.

>> Makes one wonder.

Parenthood

Parenthood—not a stream, but a torrent.
An adventure—wild, uncharted, alive.
Caring—heart-first; caressing, holding, mending.
Understanding—listening, debating, yielding.
Children—screaming, tantrums, piddling, vomiting.
Wakeful—up, down; dummies, drinks, damp sheets.
Bills—large, small, all at once, urgent and absurd.
Laughter—frequent and fierce; aching, shaking, teasing, tickling.
Mishaps—funny, foolish, fleeting, and felt.

Parenthood—a torrent that surges and subsides,
a flood of moments—messy, luminous, real.
Crying—young, old; clashing, healing, grieving, growing.
Cooking—disasters and delights; aromas that rise, tempers that fall, meals refused and remade.
Cleaning—endless; seen and unseen, the rhythm of care.
Disagreements—minor, major; sorrow, forgiveness—no winners, no losers. Compromise. Learning.
Partnerships—friendships, soul-flyers; fierce, tender, brief, forever.
Letting go while holding on.
A love stretched wider than sleep.
A journey that never ends.

Parenthood—not a stream, but a torrent.

Humility. Grace. Purpose. Being.

Red Lid

"Red lid! I heard you the first time," he calls back, rolls his eyes, and heads out the front door, plastic bag of rubbish in his hand.

Wind tunnels down the street here, makes a beeline across the cul-de-sac and whips up his long, steep, impressive driveway. Nice in summer—bugger in winter.

He walks barefoot across the concrete and squints at the morning light.

Rooooooowl.

He trips but does not fall.

His back jars—arthritis.

"Damn cat—get lost!"

He stops momentarily and marvels at the panoramic views before him. Suburbs. City. Beyond. A little smog.

    Views, because he bought the block.
    Views, because he built the house.
    Views, because he took the loan.
    Views, because he never stopped working.
        But they are *very nice views!*
Nice enough for him to *fall* into his recliner at night.
Nice enough for him to have *no* time for pleasure.
So nice that he appreciates them—
    at 7am, every Tuesday, without fail, on "red lid" day.
    "Ah, the views," he mutters proudly.

He places the bag he's carrying into the bin, but the lid won't close. It's overfull now. Such is life.

He pushes down on it and double-checks—*red lid*. Age has him questioning himself—often.

He can smell it now—seafood? But they haven't eaten seafood. Something else? His nose crinkles, and he wonders—*is that what's attracting the cat?*

He spins the bin around, grabs the handles, and starts pushing it.

Plastic wheels click rhythmically across the concrete until he reaches the crest of the driveway—clunk—clunk—clunk—clunk.
He wonders why round wheels sound square—*council's fault! Made in China, no doubt.*
His grip tightens. He must control the weighty beast—or it will drag him down.
He pushes it in front of him these days. He used to pull it behind him.
He remembers the letterbox incident. Red lid ran over him and escaped across the cul-de-sac, flattening the Joneses' letterbox and spilling its load across their lawn. The kookaburras laughed. He did not.
"Here we go again," he utters. He's off and racing—
Clunk—clunk—clunk—clunk—clunk—cl—u—u—u—u—u—nk—clunk—clunk.
He reaches the gutter. His heart slows. He breathes deeply. The stinking, plastic beast will sit on the verge until tonight, when he'll drag it back up again, emptied.
"Another load for landfill," he thinks. He always feels guilty. People should care more—leave less of a footprint on the planet.
She calls, and he instantly forgets about landfill—that's someone else's problem, anyway.
She can be loud sometimes.
"Don't forget the yellow one—both bins this week."
Shit.
He ascends his long, steep, impressive driveway, catches his breath, and readies to do it all again.
The stray cat watches his every move.
He wants to kick it. He doesn't know why.
He doesn't look at the view this time—there *is* no time, work's calling.
    Everything has a price.

Does "enough" day *ever* come?
    saved enough
        worked enough
            have enough
                done enough
                    are enough

FUN FACT: Audi (cars) is pronounced *"Ow-dee"*—like *howdy*.
Aldi (the supermarket) is pronounced *"Al-dee."*
Simple, really.
On 14 November 1899, German engineer August Horch established the company A. Horch & Cie in Cologne. This laid the foundation for the world-famous Audi brand.
Cie is the French abbreviation for *compagnie* (company).
The following poem is about the car company—not the supermarket!
I hope you enjoy this far-fetched legend as much as I enjoyed writing it.
And about the French… When we say "Excuse the French" in our household, we're not referring to our language skills—rather, to swear words. This was also what my parents said when words slipped out. History tells me it started as "excuse *my* French", but Aussies have a habit of adding a uniqueness to words, phrases and sentences.

The Legend of the Windbreaker Three

The yacht, she sailed out of Cairns,
her name—*Windbreaker Three*.
Chartered by six Germans,
from the *Audi* company.

The engineers—post-conference,
had settled on the tour.
A day trip to the Barrier Reef,
sold off a glossy brochure.

The owner of *Windbreaker Three*,
a redhead named Scott Wind.
Won her in a card game,
from a Spaniard pissed on gin.

He distributed brochures,
and employed a cut-price chef.
Flo Breezley—sole applicant,
served time for her husband's death.

Will Longbottom joined as Captain,
he brought the crew to three.
Handsome, gay and promiscuous,
he'd never been to sea!

The Windbreaker Three's first charter,
had the perfect start that day.
The Germans lazed upon the deck,
and sang along the way.

Once anchored on the pristine reef,
they snorkelled and they swam.
Each guest truly gob-smacked,
at the coral, fish, and clam.

The crew of three was lucky,
not one had checked the weather.
Distracted—dreaming of reviews,
and bookings 'hell-for-leather'.

But the sky turned black, the sea grew rough,
and the yacht began to sway.
Captain Will Googled conditions—
a cyclone was headed their way.

Scott pulled up the anchor fast,
then Will let out a shriek.
"The engine's dead—we'll have to sail.
Ewah—we're up shit creek!"

The Germans huddled below the deck,
the yacht was thrown around.
Her sails couldn't bear the force,
they tore and went sea bound.

Owner Scott dropped to his knees,
and prayed for all below.
Scott and Will-the-Captain knew,
to a watery grave they'd go.

                    Continues...

Scoffing—Flo Breezley cussed,
she'd *not* give up the ghost!
She'd make what killed her husband,
but she'd make a milder dose!

"You two can kiss your arse goodbye,
but *this* old girl's got fight.
I'll get this shit-box back to Cairns,
and I'll do it before night!"

In the low light of the galley,
Flo filled a pot with beans.
She *poured* in chilli and spices,
and called it, '*Windbreaker* Cuisine'.

She offered it to the Germans:
"Guten—meine seasick cure."
They gratefully ate with gusto.
She locked the dunny door.

The Germans' faces grimaced,
their stomachs gave a churn.
They scrambled up the ladder—
a beeline to the stern.

Six butts upon the pushpit,
unleashed an energy,
that belittled the mighty cyclone—
yacht airborne across the sea.

The cyclone tucked its eye in,
and changed direction fast.
Defeated by Flo Breezley's beans—
a savage 'cat—five' blast!

The flying yacht, with Will at helm,
crash-landed on the lawn.
Right outside of Macca's,
where this legend would be born.

The Germans, with their rears sore,
sought no compensation.
They'd found a surefire way to make
Audi a racing sensation.

Flo continued to make big bucks,
her beans now *Audi's* fuel.
Her kickback from each Grand Prix win,
made even the richest drool.

Will Longbottom, too, was offered work,
to captain the world's biggest liner.
But he turned it down in an instant,
to open his own gay diner.

Authorities seized *Windbreaker Three*,
for damages caused, and more.
Lucky Scott won another yacht,
and called her *Windbreaker Four*!

The Lump

"You'll need to see a specialist!"
Insisted my GP.
I'd pointed out a lump I have,
and tended to agree.

So, he wrote me a referral,
and I took the letter home.
Then made a prompt appointment,
via my mobile phone.

When I made my way to Adelaide,
I parked on Melbourne Street.
A colorectal surgeon,
was the specialist I'd meet.

He said, "Show me this lump of yours,
and tell me—does it hurt?"
'It's a hernia,' I told him,
then lifted up my skirt.

He started to examine me,
"Not a hernia," he said.
"I'll send you for a CT scan,
Before it starts to spread."

The next week, when the phone rang,
there was something on the scan.
I'd need a colonoscopy,
from this burly man.

So, I headed back to Adelaide—
stayed with rellies, dear.
I'd need to drink a bowel prep,
to make my poop run clear.

I made the prep—a jug full,
my procedure—the next day.
Their Labrador downed the bloody lot,
when I briefly looked away.

I ducked out—bought a second pack,
and made the prep again.
I started drinkin' after five,
and shittin' after ten.

The dog and I took turns that night,
at runnin' to the loo.
'til on the couch, I fell asleep,
and the ruddy dog did too.

George the chocolate Lab and I,
sat dozing side by side.
Exhausted—blissfully unaware,
of a mess we couldn't hide.

Liquid poop—full of bits,
had soaked the dog and me.
My clothes, his hair, the couch, the floor,
a poo catastrophe!

After the colonoscopy,
the specialist phoned again.
"You'll never guess what we found,
It's a hernia, my friend!"

Continues…

I didn't need the colonoscopy
—his camera up my crack.
That colorectal surgeon,
can give my money back!

FUN FACT: cyclones and hurricanes are the same thing. What they're called depends on which part of the world you live in. In the Southern Hemisphere, they spin in a clockwise direction. In the Northern Hemisphere, they spin anticlockwise.

In March 1997, I was living on the northern beaches of Cairns when Category 3 Cyclone Justin passed over our heads. The first part of the cyclone battered us with strong southerly winds and horizontal rain. The kids were entertained by trees bending like elastic and banging against power lines in our street. The sparks were explosive.

The second part of the cyclone brought wind and rain from the north. The change in direction happens because cyclones spiral, and by this time, the ground is so sodden that the force on tree roots can and does uproot them.

During the eye—it passed right over us—we ventured outside. The sky was clear—eerily so—and there was no wind. It gives a false sense of calm. With Justin, it was toward the end of the cyclone that the power went out—generator time.

If you've never been through a cyclone, it's hard to imagine just how uncomfortable they are. The wind is warm, the humidity oppressive, and when the power fails, you'd sell your children for a fan! We discovered paint doesn't dry either!

Post-cyclone, the cleanup begins. Muck is stuck to your house windows and walls—from horizontal wind and rain—and sets like concrete. Of course, the water supply fails with intakes clogged with debris, so there's no hosing anything off. There's also flooding, cutting highways and stopping transport. Supermarkets sell out and their shelves remain bare!

Cyclones are a mighty force—and a powerful reminder that, as humans, nature belittles us.

The Power of Wind

Imagine living life without the wind—or a fresh breeze.
No pollen drifting high or low to aggravate a sneeze.
No floral scents floating by, drawing insects near.
No dispersing flatulence when you've drunk too much beer!

No wafting dog pheromones at 'reproduction time'.
Think about what Earth would be without the canine kind!
Shifting sand would cease to move, leaves silent on their bough.
Pollination… Reproduction… Rely on wind somehow!

We'd be without the flowers. We'd be without the bees.
And we'd all be pretty grumpy without a summer breeze!
What would move the winter clouds and let the sunshine through?
What would bring the summer clouds and keep us shaded, too?

Life without strong wind, I wonder, how would old trees fall?
Forests would grow dense, and we would not get through at all.
Wind brings with it damage, creating work for human masses.
Some rely on cyclones just to pay their bloody taxes!

There'd be no breeze to windsurf or sail the oceans through.
No wafting morning coffee smells or scents of tasty stew.
Wind *is* a trivial topic to the unappreciative mind,
but consider life without it and the effect upon mankind!

life is a continuum
    people, places, animals, experiences
        forgettable, unforgettable
            minuscule, monumental
                never pointless

NEVER POINTLESS

Veronica—*Things Life Gave You*

Veronica—

Parents gave you: *life—siblings—education.*
Genetics gave you: *beauty—blue eyes—blonde hair.*
Youth gave you: *dreams—enthusiasm—excitement.*
Love gave you: *longing—passion—direction.*
Marriage brought you: *children—tears—laughter.*
Children gave you: *reason—purpose—workload.*

And then—

Reality brought you: *heartache—desperation—divorce.*
Faith gave you: *healing—clarity—humility.*
Time offered you: *wisdom—forgiveness—strength.*
Experience gave you: *knowledge—understanding—perspective.*
Patience gave you: *opportunity—unity—harmony.*
Fate dealt you: *Motor Neurone Disease.*

Life gives and life takes away.

MND *silenced your voice—betrayed your body—claimed your days—*
but the bastard underestimated you—it *could not* steal your smile!

Rest in peace, my beautiful friend—
these were the things life gave you.

Birds have wings—we clip them.
      People have hearts—we crush them.
The world has colour—we drain it.
      Our minds are endless—we close them.

Unmoored—
A Hot Air Balloon Trip Reflection

Giant bird with nylon wings,
and breast of woven cane.
Unmoor me from this rooted earth,
and fill my mind again.

As darkness slowly leaves the earth,
so ghostly, without sound.
While morning dew disintegrates,
as sunlight warms the ground.

To see the mountain shadows wake,
and stretch to meet the morn.
Beneath the parting whisps of cloud,
where colored skies are born.

To heights where trees resemble peas,
and farming plots—a quilt.
These speckled shades of green and brown—
the Lord's paint palette, spilt.

Giant bird with nylon wings,
and breast of woven cane.
You showed me a horizon,
and eased my tethered chain.

Each morning is a painting—
there's never one the same.
Each sunrise is the picture,
each ballooning trip, the frame.

Without cold, how can we appreciate warmth?
Without hunger, how can we appreciate food?
Without loss, how can we appreciate life?

COLD / WARMTH HUNGER / FOOD LOSS / LIFE

  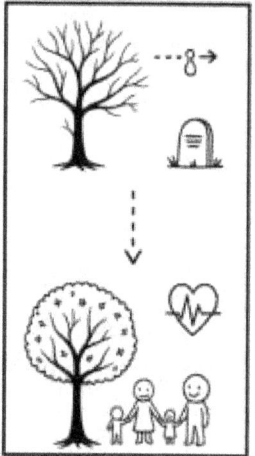

WITHOUT ONE, HOW CAN WE APPRECIATE THE OTHER?

Winter at the Station

I stiffen. My nose tip burns, my earlobes ache—it's bitterly cold.
Wind swirls, directionless, funnelled by concrete walls.
I shiver, hands deep in shallow pockets—little comfort.

I listen. The noise around me hypnotises—whir, whine, whiz.
Eardrums hum, static, the sound of unconscious listening,
I focus, individual sounds dissolve into white noise.

I push. I am pushed by the hustle and bustle—eyes slide through me.
Footsteps surround, scurrying, walking, running, stepping,
I breathe, my head and feet throb—destination home.

I blink. Fumes fill my nose and sting my eyes—I rub them.
Tears pool, escaping, running, dripping, falling.
I watch, salty droplets on diesel-slickened ground—soaking into chaos.

I squint. Fluorescent tubes imitate sunlight—I ponder.
My shadow lacks distinction, fading, here even light feels borrowed.

I sense,
    this place is only a passage,
        life a station in winter—
            we pass through,
                carrying our shadow,
                    until it leaves us.

The Dunlop Volley Odes

The Dunlop Volley Odes began in 1996.

At this time, the RAAF Scherger Base was being constructed east of Weipa, a town on Cape York Peninsula in Far North Queensland.

The location is approximately an 800-kilometre drive from Cairns, and in the 1990s, much of it was an unsealed road. The drive was as dusty, hot and rugged as the destination.

My husband Marty and I lived in Cairns. Marty—a commercial roofer for many decades—was part of a small team that accepted a contract to sheet the RAAF hangars. The sheets were to be laid in a camouflage pattern made up from four different-coloured Colorbond sheets. RAAF provided the pattern.

The first day on the roof was chaos. The boys had worn and relied on Dunlop Volleys shoes for years. Their rubber soles were perfect on the roof and gripped like no other shoes. For this contract, the boys would be away for months, so they all bought new Volleys to take away with them to last the distance.

From the moment they first stepped on the roof, they knew they were in trouble—slipping and sliding all over the roof sheets. They studied their Volleys and discovered that the design had been changed. Dunlop had reinvented the shoe, changing the sole from rubber to synthetic, and the grip was no more.

Back in Cairns, I received a phone call—a cry for help from the boys. I had to drive around the city, visit each of their homes, and collect and box up their half-worn Volley shoes—the old ones with rubber soles. *This was not a pleasant task considering how much feet sweat in a tropical environment!* I immediately shipped them to Weipa.

Marty insisted I get in touch with Dunlop and ask them what was going on with their ever-reliable shoe. I decided I would put pen to paper and write to the General Manager of Dunlop Footwear from my heart—humorously and poetically—and send the boys' concerns by fax. The first poem—one of five poems I was to write on the subject, *Ode to a Dunlop Volley* was sent on 17.12.1996.

Our team consisted of: Rusty, Kozzo, Jacko, Marko, Jamie, Marty, and Kenny. Some of the boys' names have been changed from the original poems to respect their privacy today. Otherwise, apart from a couple of English and flow corrections, these poems remain mostly unchanged.

Ode to a Dunlop Volley

To our dearest Mr Dunlop, what is it you have done
to our famous Volley shoes, we thought were number one?

We didn't notice a change in tread on brand-new pairs we bought,
to take to work in Weipa town for contracts newly sought.

We couldn't use our Volleys—they didn't fare too well.
First time upon the roofing iron, we slipped and darn near fell!

See, aircraft hangars—twelve in all—designed for camouflaging,
guarantee an undie change, when to the edge, you're charging!

Clinging to the gutter tight, we cried suggestive words,
and prayed the Dunlop company would note them if they heard.

Alas, we ain't no angels, true, if so, we wouldn't flown.
Instead, we rang the missus fast, "Send our old Volleys from home!"

Well, the job got done with lots of sweat—our old shoes held up well.
Problem is, now back in Cairns, they've rot and gained a smell.

For 16 years we've worn your shoes, we buy a pair bimonthly.
All roofers in Australia know they're all that's safe and comfy.

So, we beg you, Mr Dunlop, Sir, have mercy on our "soles",
and put the grip back instantly to Dunlop Volley moulds.

For if you don't, no jobs we'll have—we can't stand on the roof.
For compromise, there ain't no shoe, and that's the darndest truth.

So, if you have old stock at hand, please send at breakneck pace—
to save us blokes an accident—a footpath in the face!

Regards, Marty (size 12), Jamie, and Kozzo (size 10).

The General Manager at Dunlop Footwear wrote back to us on the same day—also by fax—with a note and poem in response.

The GM's note said that he would try to get the boys a pair of the old rubber-soled Volley in their sizes. He apologised for the problem and advised us they'd be back in full stock by March or April of 1997. It appeared—according to the GM—he had no idea the Volley was the preferred roofing shoe for Australian roofers, and they'd had *many* complaints.

The poem he penned was a great effort—rhyming and all! He titled it, "Ye Olde Volley". It stated that although they were Mexicans down south, they'd heard the complaints loud and clear from around Australia. He went on to say his attempt at reinventing the shoe had failed, and his job was on the line; I never worked out whether he was serious or not! He jokes about having a time frame to fix his error and for us to be patient while they deal with the problem. Also, he promises to send us old models (rubber soled) in our sizes until the shoes are back in shops.

The boys remained patient, but the shoes didn't come. It was time for another poem. This one was faxed 02.03.1997

Ode to a Missing Volley

Our dearest Mr Dunlop, where is it they have gone—
those Volleys shoes you promised us on Marty's mobile phone?

You said you'd send them urgently; we didn't hold our breath.
Damn good job we didn't, too—be nothin' of us left!

There's trouble here in Cairns right now, the dole queue's makin' room.
Boss Kenny's feelin' nauseous, "bare feet," he says, "won't do!"

The posty won't deliver our mail—he's scared of bein' beat.
He let it slip he had a pair—"old models" on his feet.

Even grandpa on the corner put a mean dog in his yard.
Didn't think he'd see the day—he'd have old shoes to guard.

Joggers are joggin' faster too, in efforts to curb a bashin'.
Nobody's goin' out alone in Volleys—a risky fashion.

Shoe stores are lockin' up it seems, when roofers come to call.
It's chancy sayin' "Sorry, Sir, the factory seems to've stalled!"

"It's sad to see ol' Marty cry," I told me next-door neighbour.
"Hope they send them Volleys quick and stop his rash behaviour!"

Continues...

Our sex-life's gone to ruins too—he brings old Volleys to bed.
And guards them there obsessively—under the pillow near his head!
Though cyclones may pass closely by and monsoon rains immerse us,

there ain't no problem big as havin' a gang of Volley-less roofers!

So, Mr Dunlop get your crew to take a second look,
for Volleys of the old model and send by hook or crook!

We'll even pay—don't ask for much—we're desperate, can't you see?
And Marty says he'll trade me in for old size twelve Volley.

From Marty's desperate missus.

Time passed. We didn't see the return of the rubber-soled Volley shoes. The boys found it very hard to find shoes with rubber soles, and when they did, they were expensive and didn't last long for the price. Two of the boys clocked up accidents—I'm not saying it was anyone's fault, but it was time for another poem, regardless. This was faxed 17.12.1997

Ode to a Volley's Twilight Hour

You said you'd send us Volleys, well, we reckon that you lied.
'cause we've been waitin' twelve months plus and still they ain't arrived.

Now things have changed since poems last, they've gone beyond a joke.
Our roofin' team just can't afford to lose another bloke.

T'was Jamie first, four flights up, went sliding off the gutter.
Left sections of his hairy legs on scaffold—spread like butter!

They stitched him up; the crabs missed out on human thigh as bait.
He blamed his fall on dying Volleys, "They got no grip left, mate!"

Marko was next to take a plunge—two stories was his dive.
The doctors said, "The lucky bastard shouldn't be alive!"

Three weeks plus on life support, and now that he's awake, says, "T'was me worn out Volley shoes that damn near sealed me fate!"

Big Marty, in his fossilised shoes, to date is death-plunge free, but summer's seen his feet sure shrink—wafer-soled Volley fricassee.

So, poems I write to save their heads; to find some shoes with grip.
They need your Dunlop Volleys, Sir, the rubber-soled ones— quick.

Continues...

I pray you have them now in stock, it's ages since I wrote.

If not, then simply tell us please, where rubber soles are bought?

The new Dunlop Classic Volley finally returned to the shops. The boys were delighted. The following poem was faxed with thanks on 30.07.1998

Ode to the Resurrection of the Gripping Volley

Us roofers are celebratin' and it ain't the boss that's tops.
We're just thrilled to buggery, with "Classics" back in shops.

The grip we've missed for near two years has come back from the dead,
resurrected in "Classic" shoes, thanks to the things we said.

There ain't a shoe that's like it, it's a fashion statement, see.
On building sites, and sporting fields, and going out for tea.

So, we thought we'd drop a line to you—tell you how we're doin'.
We're grippin' to the sheets again—we're layin' and we're screwin'.

Our Marty's smilin', back on top—his missus in the sack.
He's sleepin' in new "Classics"—put the old ones out the back!

His dog's impressed, he's realised, his bones just have no taste,
compared to fossilised Volley shoes he dug out of their waste.

Our Jamie's thinkin' marriage, hmm, to Blondie—well, we'll see.
Reckons he'll look handsome with a tux and new Volleys.

"Jacko's choofin'", says his neighbour. "That smell's back like before!"
But the smell's his Dunlop Volleys—it's his "Classics" by the door.

Continues...

Kozzo's never worried much, 'bout fallin' off the roof.
"Me hair'll save me—all three feet of dreads and matted roots!"

Boss, Kenny's got a problem, even though his feet have grip
It's through his slimy fingers that all the women slip.

Rusty exchanged his kid's sandshoes—put small-size "Classics" on.
They say, "small feet, small you-know-what", well, Rusty proves them wrong!

Marko's missus pulled his life-support—slipped on new "Classics" shoes,
then dragged him out of ICU, she'd heard the awesome news.

"They've put the grip back, Marko-love—in Volleys, that's the truth.
So, take your drip and urine bag and get back on the roof!"

As you see, our lives have changed, but really, we can't moan,
'cause we've got grip and shouldn't slip—let's hope it's our final poem!

But it wasn't our final poem…

We were promised a pair of Volley Classics each in exchange for a photoshoot (organised by Royce Communications and shot by The Cairns Post), and the permission to use these poems at a launch for the Dunlop Volley Classic Shoes in Melbourne. The following final poem was faxed 28.10.1998

Ode to Roofers Too Sexy for their Volleys

They've not yet received their Volleys, but they've gained a sexual aura,
sought now for their model looks from Cooktown out to Laura.

They're famous down in Melbourne, too, since photos hit the street.
Modellin' Dunlop Volley shoes—new Classics on their feet.

The boys call it an omen—say they've been in the wrong trade,
and if women like the rough look, then for certain, they'll get laid.

Marty—I've been beggin' him, "Love, please don't quit your job—
got bills for liposuction and your extended 'thingamabob!'

Jamie—stalks the postman and it ain't for Volleys, free.
It's his million-dollar contract modellin' G-strings by the sea.

Kozzo—his debts are mountin'; got a rug rat on the way.
He's workin' as a hair model—for anti-headlice spray!

Jacko—his jobs are stallin'; safety officer in a bind.
He's roofin' with no clothes on—flawless suntan on *his* mind!

Marko—he's back in the ward—a model for intensive care.
Latest styles in hospice gowns with matching underwear.

Continues...

Rusty—he's talkin' modelin' too; beer products, I heard him mutter.
Hats, coolers and XXXX shirts while rollin' in the gutter.

Kenny—hair all matted—struck a pose down by the beach.
Council mistook him for a stray, and stuck him on a leash.

Alas, Wet Season's 'bout to start, and roofless buildings grow.
Send the shoes you promised us, and back to work they'll go.

Why? Because they're freebies and with freebies on their feet, they'll forget the blasted modellin' bit and bring home food to eat.

Regards, Marty's desperate missus—*again!*

We did get our free Volley Classic Shoes and wore them out. We also received photos from our photo shoot in Cairns. Sadly, after two major accidents coming off unforgiving roofs, we lost Marko to Leukaemia in 2023. RIP Marko. The rest of the tradie boys—now in their late 50s and early 60s—are still kickin' as I write this. Jacko and Rusty are still roofing. Kenny is still the boss—long in the tooth and overdue for retirement. Kozzo's gone bush. Jamie's working in safety. And Marty… he's retired post-heart and spinal surgery, having worn his body out in an unforgiving trade. These blokes were—and still are—some of the toughest characters in Australia. Anyone who works outdoors in the tropical heat of Cairns or in Northern Australia—particularly in the summer months—is one hell of a machine and deserves a whole lot of respect.

Thank you for reading—

my quotes, my poems, my explanations and my fun facts.
There's a piece of my heart in every letter,
and a piece of my life in every word.

Heather Jane Hill

About the Author

Heather Jane Hill is an Australian writer who divides her time between Tropical North Queensland and South Australia's Yorke Peninsula, where she lives with her husband and two much-loved staffies. A proud country girl, art enthusiast, nurse, and former tour guide, she draws endless inspiration from the rhythms of everyday life, the beauty of the natural world, and the complexities of human nature. After honing her skills writing for the tourism industry, she leapt into independent publishing, creating works across multiple genres, including novels, poetry, young adult fiction, and children's picture books.

Other Books available

My Kids' rhyming short story books...

- *The Termi'rific Haircut*
- *The Seymour Big-Cloud Strut*
- *The Quickest Quokka's Quest*

Poetry for Kids'...

- *The Baker's Dozen. 13 Critter Poems from Northern Australia*

My Debut Rural Romance Novel

- *June's March...*

She came to Millbrook for a quiet country locum—for the month of March, nothing more. She got a hormonal turkey, a steer with attitude... and a meddlesome grandma with matchmaking on her mind.

June's not exactly a country girl—so house-sitting a menagerie of wayward animals in Tropical North Queensland is not what she signed up for. Still, she's determined to make it work, even if the local wildlife (and a surgery full of trying characters) seem intent on testing her sanity.

Enter Dave: rugged, reserved, annoyingly attractive—and clearly not over his past. But Dave's gran has plans, and subtlety isn't one of them. As June gets drawn deeper into the rhythm of small-town life, she discovers that the animals aren't the only ones with wild hearts.

www.ingramcontent.com/pod-product-compliance
Lightning Source LLC
Chambersburg PA
CBHW071843290426
44109CB00017B/1905